HEROES OF NATIVE AMERICAN HISTORY

THE LIFE OF TECUMSEH

DONNA REYNOLDS

PowerKiDS press

Published in 2024 by The Rosen Publishing Group, Inc.
2544 Clinton Street, Buffalo, NY 14224

Portions of this work were originally authored by Walter LaPlante and published as *Tecumseh*. All new material in this edition was authored by Donna Reynolds.

Editor: Jennifer Lombardo
Book Design: Rachel Rising

Photo Credits: Cover, p. 1 Tecumseh/B. & E. sc.; S.W./LOC, pp. 4, 6, 8, 10, 12, 14, 16, 18, 20 Vector1st/Shutterstock.com; p. 5 https://commons.wikimedia.org/wiki/File:Henry_Lovie_-_View_of_Bald_Face_Creek_in_the_Ohio_River_Valley_-_Google_Art_Project.jpg; p. 7 https://commons.wikimedia.org/wiki/File:Tecumseh02.jpg; p. 9 https://commons.wikimedia.org/wiki/File:Treaty_of_Greenville.jpg; p. 11 https://commons.wikimedia.org/wiki/File:Tens-kwau-ta-waw,_the_prophet.jpg; p.13 https://commons.wikimedia.org/wiki/File:Entrance_P4190114_Prophetstown_SP,_Battleground.jpg; p. 15 https://commons.wikimedia.org/wiki/File:Battle_of_Tippecanoe_LCCN2003656861.jpg; p. 17 https://commons.wikimedia.org/wiki/File:Meeting_of_Brock_and_Tecumseh,_1812.jpg; p.19 https://commons.wikimedia.org/wiki/File:William_Henry_Harrison.jpg; p. 21 Prachaya Roekdeethaweesab/Shutterstock.com.

Library of Congress Cataloging-in-Publication Data
Names: Reynolds, Donna.
Title: The life of tecumseh / Donna Reynolds
Description: New York : Powerkids Press, 2024. | Series: Heroes of native american history | Includes glossary, index, and bibliographic information
Identifiers: ISBN 9781642825367 (pbk) | ISBN 9781642825374 (library bound) | ISBN 9781642825381 (ebook)
Subjects: LCSH: Indigenous people–United States– Juvenile literature | Shawnee Indians– Juvenile literature| United States–History–War of 1812– Juvenile literature
Classification: LCC E99.S35 R46 2024 | DDC 920.0092/97-dc24

Manufactured in the United States of America

CPSIA Compliance Information: Batch #CSPK24. For Further Information contact Rosen Publishing at 1-800-237-9932.

CONTENTS

The Birth of Tecumseh

Tecumseh was born around 1768 in the Ohio River Valley. Tecumseh's father, a Shawnee, was killed by white men. His mother, a Muskogee, went to live in Missouri when Tecumseh was seven years old. Tecumseh was raised by his sister and a Shawnee chief named Blackfish.

Ohio River Valley

The Power of Words

Because of his father's murder and other **cruel** actions by white Americans, Tecumseh didn't like white people. However, he didn't want to treat them the way they treated his people. Tecumseh **convinced** the Shawnee to avoid being cruel to white people. He learned his words could have power.

Speaking Against Selling

In 1795, some Native American chiefs, including Tecumseh, gathered to talk about selling their land to the U.S. government. When the other chiefs signed the **treaty**, Tecumseh was angry. He said it wasn't their land to sell. It belonged to all Native Americans.

Prophetstown

Tecumseh's brother Tenskwatawa became a famous **religious** leader. Other Native Americans called him the **Prophet**. In 1808, Tecumseh traveled to join him. Together, they created a place called Prophetstown where Native Americans could come to talk about resisting the Europeans.

Tecumseh and Tenskwatawa spoke against the U.S. government taking more of their homelands. Tecumseh traveled around the country speaking to other groups about the problem, trying to convince them to join Prophetstown. He wanted all Native Americans to work together.

Prophetstown
State Park

Beaten by Harrison

While Tecumseh was away in 1811, General William Henry Harrison camped near Prophetstown. Tenskwatawa led the Shawnee against Harrison's forces in what's now called the Battle of Tippecanoe. Tenskwatawa lost and then moved to Canada. He couldn't help Tecumseh with his plans after that.

The War of 1812

The War of 1812 was fought between Great Britain and the United States. Tecumseh decided to join the fight. He gathered a group of followers who wanted to travel to Canada with him to fight alongside the British.

Tecumseh and his followers played an important part in the British taking Detroit. However, not long after, U.S. soldiers led by General Harrison pushed the British back into Canada. During the Battle of the Thames in October 1813, Tecumseh was killed.

William Henry Harrison

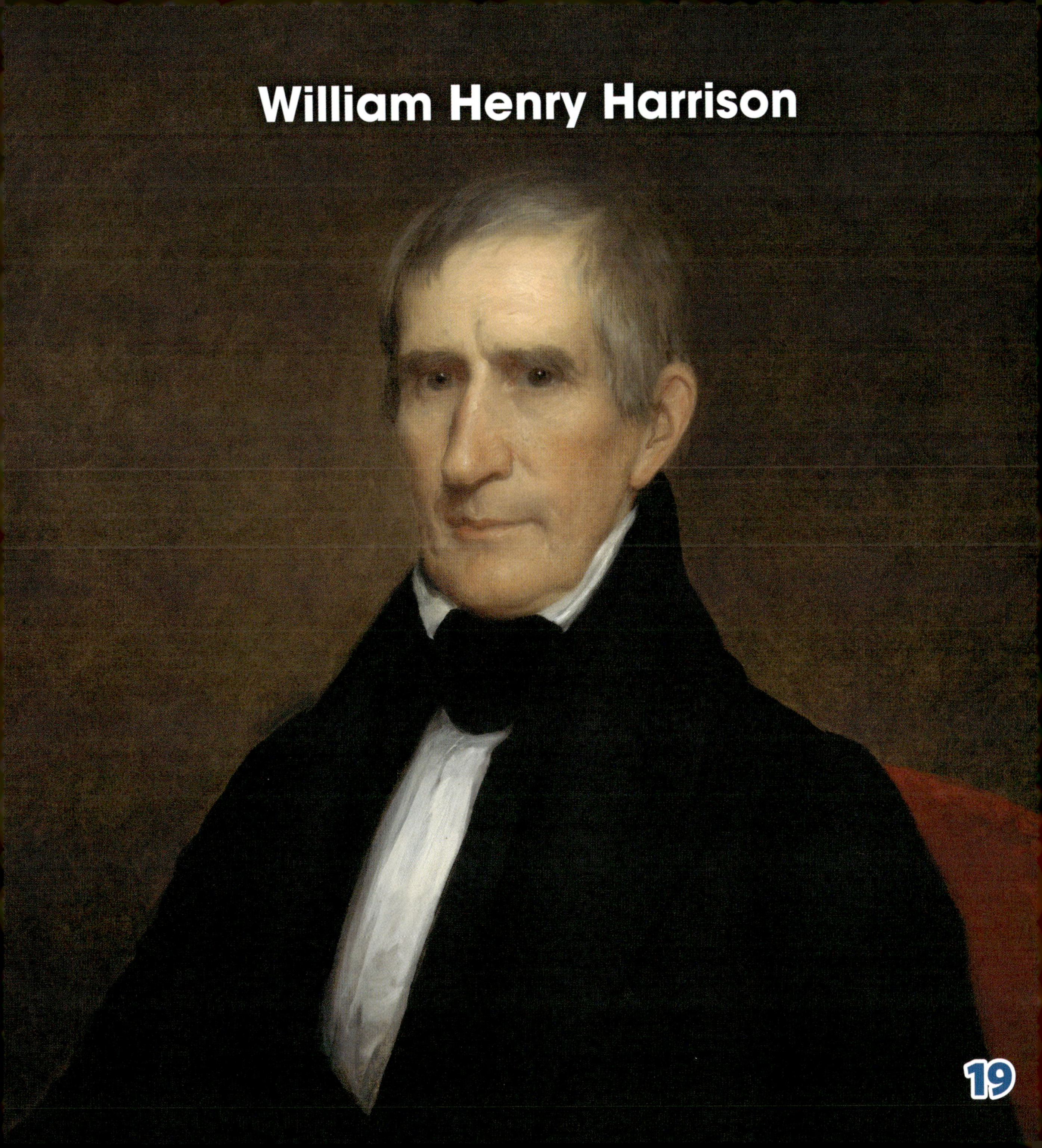

A Hero Forever

No one ever found out who killed Tecumseh or where his body was buried. After he died, many other Shawnee stopped fighting. The government forced them to move to Oklahoma. Today, Natives and non-Natives alike remember the Shawnee hero Tecumseh.

GLOSSARY

convince: To argue so as to make a person agree or believe.

cruel: Wanting to cause others to suffer.

prophet: Someone who declares publicly a message that they believe has come from God or a god.

religious: Relating to faith in a god or gods.

treaty: An agreement between groups of people.

FOR MORE INFORMATION

BOOKS

Kinew, Wab, and Joe Morse. *Go Show the World: A Celebration of Indigenous Heroes*. Toronto, ON: Tundra Books, 2018.

Micklos, John, and Rhonda Dass. *Tecumseh: Get to Know the Shawnee Chief Who Fought to Protect Native Lands*. North Mankato, MN: Capstone Press, 2019.

WEBSITES

Britannica Kids: Shawnee
kids.britannica.com/kids/article/Shawnee/353767
Read about Tecumseh's people, the Shawnee.

History for Kids: Tecumseh
www.historyforkids.net/tecumseh.html
Learn more about Tecumseh's life.

Publisher's note to educators and parents: Our editors have carefully reviewed these websites to ensure that they are suitable for students. Many websites change frequently, however, and we cannot guarantee that a site's future contents will continue to meet our high standards of quality and educational value. Be advised that students should be closely supervised whenever they access the internet.

INDEX